Building the Panama Canal

Sabrina Crewe and Dale Anderson

Gareth Stevens Publishing

A WORLD ALMANAC EDUCATION GROUP COMPANY

Please visit our web site at: www.garethstevens.com
For a free color catalog describing Gareth Stevens Publishing's list of high-quality
books and multimedia programs, call 1-800-542-2595 (USA) or 1-800-387-3178
(Canada). Gareth Stevens Publishing's fax: (414) 332-3567.

Library of Congress Cataloging-in-Publication Data

Crewe, Sabrina.
    Building the Panama Canal / by Sabrina Crewe and Dale Anderson.
      p. cm. — (Events that shaped America)
    Includes bibliographical references and index.
    ISBN 0-8368-3413-5 (lib. bdg.)
    1. Panama Canal (Panama)—History—Juvenile literature. 2. Canals—Panama—
Design and construction—History—Juvenile literature. 3. Canal Zone—History—
Juvenile literature. I. Anderson, Dale, 1953-. II. Title. III. Series.
    F1569.C2C74 2005
    972.87'3—dc22   2004057895

This North American edition first published in 2005 by
Gareth Stevens Publishing
A WRC Media Company
330 West Olive Street, Suite 100
Milwaukee, WI 53212 USA

This edition © 2005 by Gareth Stevens Publishing.

Produced by Discovery Books
Editor: Sabrina Crewe
Designer and page production: Sabine Beaupré
Photo researcher: Sabrina Crewe
Maps and diagrams: Stefan Chabluk
Gareth Stevens editorial direction: Mark J. Sachner
Gareth Stevens editor: Monica Rausch
Gareth Stevens art direction: Tammy West
Gareth Stevens production: Jessica Morris

Photo credits: Corbis: cover, pp. 5, 9, 10, 13, 17, 18, 20 (both), 21, 23, 25, 26;
Library of Congress: pp. 12, 15, 16 (both), 19, 22, 24; North Wind Picture
Archives: pp. 6, 7, 8, 11, 14.

Printed in the United States of America

1 2 3 4 5 6 7 8 9 09 08 07 06 05

Contents

Introduction

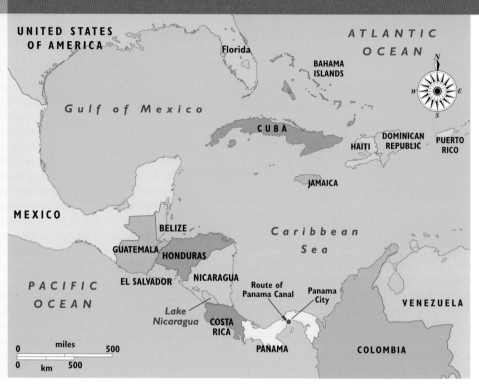

You can see on this map that Panama forms a narrow bridge between North and South America.

The Isthmus

The country of Panama is part of an isthmus, which is a narrow strip of land connecting two larger landmasses. This particular isthmus links the North American continent (which includes Central America) with the South American continent. What makes Panama especially important is the fact that it is narrower than any other part of Central America. In Panama, just a thin strip of land separates the Pacific Ocean from the Atlantic Ocean.

A Huge Challenge

For several hundred years, people tried to figure out how to connect the two oceans with a **canal** big enough for ships to sail through. Until the early 1900s, however, they didn't have the money and **technology** to do it. In the 1880s, a French company worked on a canal in Panama, but the project failed. In 1905, the U.S. government began to build a canal in Panama. This time, the project was successful.

It took tens of thousands of workers to build the Panama Canal, which runs about 50 miles (80 kilometers) across the isthmus to connect the Atlantic and Pacific Oceans. The canal finally opened in 1914.

The Reason to Build

Why did people build this huge canal? Using the canal, ships can save about 9,000 miles (14,500 km) on the journey from New York City to San Francisco because they no longer have to go around the southern tip of South America. Ships going between Europe and Asia save thousands of miles, too. Many ships, carrying millions of tons of cargo, use the canal every year to shorten their journeys.

An Important Historic Event
"The creation of the Panama Canal was far more than a vast, unprecedented feat of engineering. It was a profoundly important historic event and a sweeping human drama. . . . It marked a score of advances in engineering, government planning, [and] labor relations. . . . And yet the passage of the first ship through the canal . . . marked the resolution of a dream as old as the voyages of Columbus."

David McCullough, The Path Between the Seas, *1977*

A 2002 photograph of the Panama Canal shows vessels of all sizes on the busy route.

Chapter One

Trying to Bridge the Oceans

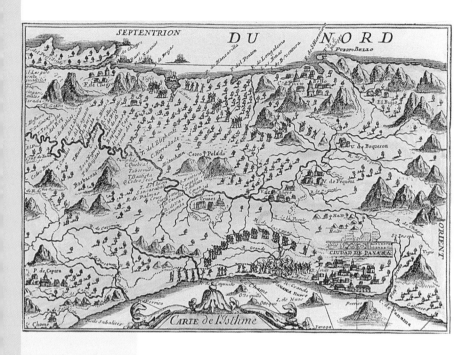

A 1744 map shows the forests and mountains that make up Panama. The landscape was a challenge to people hoping to build a canal there.

Conquering the Americas

The story of the Panama Canal begins with the Spanish exploration of the Americas in the early 1500s. At this time, Spain conquered Mexico and Peru, gaining rich gold and silver mines. The Spanish made the Native peoples of those countries mine the silver and gold, which the Spanish then took back to Spain. To get it to Spain, Peru's silver had to be transported across dense forests to the Caribbean Sea or loaded on ships in the Pacific and carried around the southern tip of South America. Both routes were long and dangerous, and Spanish officials began talking about building a canal across Central America.

Talk but No Action

In the end, the Spanish did not build a canal, but in the early 1800s, various other people raised the idea once again. Some drew up imaginative plans, but still no canal was built. No one could agree on a plan or raise the huge sums of money needed to carry out the work.

The United States Gets Involved

In the mid-1800s, some U.S. leaders began promoting the idea of a transportation route that would cut across Central America. At the time, there were no railroads that crossed the whole of the United States, and it was many years before cars, trucks, and airplanes would carry people and goods from east to west. People relied heavily on ships for transportation, and they wanted to speed up the journey from the Atlantic to the Pacific and back.

The Panama Railroad Company

In 1846, the U.S. government signed a **treaty** with Colombia, which controlled Panama. This agreement gave the United States the right to carry people and goods across Panama.

Efforts to build a canal however, went nowhere. So several American businessmen formed the Panama Railroad Company in 1847, aiming to build a railroad link instead. They ran into many problems, and only 7 miles (11 km) of track were laid before the company ran out of money.

Before the Panama Canal was built, people traveling by ship from one side of North America to the other had to go thousands of miles south and then north again. In the 1800s, that journey took many months.

The Gold Rush

Meanwhile, Americans found a new reason to travel west. In early 1848, gold was found in California. The discovery encouraged thousands of people to go to California, hoping to strike it rich. Many traveled overland across North America, while others took ships around the tip of South America. Some tried to cut the journey short by crossing the isthmus of Panama.

Crossing Panama

Although traveling across Panama cut thousands of miles from their trip, the gold seekers who crossed the isthmus found it a difficult and dangerous journey. The first stretch, from the coast by boat down the Chagres River, was not so bad. The rest of the trip, however, had to be

Travelers make the journey through the Panama jungle.

made by horse or mule through 50 miles (80 km) of steep mountain passes and dense jungle. At one point, camels were brought from Africa to carry people across Panama. Many people caught tropical diseases, such as malaria and yellow fever, and died. Bayard Taylor, a journalist who wrote about the Gold Rush, described the Panama jungle: "The only sounds in that leafy wilderness were the chattering of monkeys as they cracked the palm nuts and the scream of parrots, flying from tree to tree."

Too Many Emigrants

"There were about seven hundred emigrants waiting for passage, when I reached Panama. All the tickets the steamer could possibly receive had been issued and so great was the anxiety to get on, that double price, $600, was frequently paid for a ticket to San Francisco."

Bayard Taylor, Eldorado, *1850*

The sudden demand for transportation gave the Panama Railroad's owners new hope. Soon the company raised funds to complete the railroad, which was finished in 1855. Until the end of the 1860s, the railroad carried thousands of people across Panama.

Looking for a Project

Americans were not the only people looking to improve the route across Panama. Ferdinand de Lesseps from France had masterminded the construction of the 100-mile (160-km) Suez Canal in North Africa. In the 1870s, he was looking for a new project and eventually settled on the idea of a Central American canal.

The Panama Railroad ran 49 miles (79 km) from the Caribbean coast to Panama City on the Pacific coast. In addition to passengers, it carried cargo traveling from Asia to Europe or the United States.

On his arrival in Panama, de Lesseps was greeted in Panama City by huge crowds under a triumphal arch with his picture at the top.

Dying Like Animals

"It was the same way — bury, bury, bury, running two, three, and four trains a day with dead [workers] all the time. I never saw anything like it. It did not matter . . . whether they were black or white, to see the way they died there. They died like animals."

S. W. Plume, recalling the deaths of canal workers in Panama, 1902

The Problems Start

De Lesseps raised money in France to begin construction. He bought the Panama Railroad so he could use it to move men, supplies, and **debris** during the canal project.

Work on the canal began in 1880, but problems arose almost immediately. First, de Lesseps wanted to dig a sea-level canal, so he wouldn't have to put in **locks**. Some of the route crossed very high land, however, so workers had to dig a long way down through hundreds of feet of rock to get to sea level.

Battling the Jungle

In addition, Panama's jungle and swamps were difficult to move through. These warm, wet areas were also perfect breeding grounds for mosquitoes, which carried the germs that cause malaria and yellow fever. These deadly diseases killed as many as twenty thousand workers and weakened thousands more.

Panama Plagues

Both yellow fever and malaria are caused by tiny germs that are injected into the human body when a mosquito bites a person. Within a few days, a yellow fever victim begins to suffer headache, backache, high fever, and nausea. People with yellow fever often die within a week of showing symptoms. Malaria is less likely to kill its victims, but it makes them too sick to work, and symptoms can come back years later. At the time the French were working on the Panama Canal, doctors did not understand the connection between mosquitoes and either disease, and so they didn't know how to prevent people from getting sick.

Sick workers, heavy rains, and mud and rock slides greatly slowed the work. By late 1888, there was not enough money to continue. In 1889, the French canal company gave up and declared **bankruptcy**.

The French canal team worked hard, but they fought sickness, mud slides, and other problems.

The American Plan

Looking Abroad

By the late 1800s, the United States had built a railroad that could carry people and goods quickly from its east coast to the west coast. American leaders, however, still wanted to find a way for ships to travel more quickly between the Atlantic and Pacific Oceans. The United States now controlled islands in the Pacific, including Hawaii and the Philippines, and it also wanted to trade with countries in the Far East.

Americans wanted to build a canal, but they were concerned about the high death rate during the French project. A 1904 magazine illustrated that concern with a cover showing "Death" hovering over Panama.

Renewed Enthusiasm

So Americans were once more interested in a canal across Central America—but where? In 1899, Congress formed a committee to compare the route begun in Panama with a new route through Nicaragua. Many members of Congress preferred the Nicaragua route.

This route had a huge lake in the middle, which would reduce the amount of digging needed. Disease was also less of a problem in Nicaragua. Plus, the Panama route was already marked by the failure of the French effort.

In 1902, however, the U.S. government decided on the Panama route. It was largely convinced by a French engineer named Philippe Bunau-Varilla. He persuaded the owners of the French equipment and existing work to sell their interests to the United States for $40 million.

Philippe Bunau-Varilla (1859–1940)

Philippe Bunau-Varilla was the driving force behind the plan to build a canal across Panama. This photograph shows him on the Panama Canal in 1914, two days before its grand opening.

Philippe Bunau-Varilla trained in France as an engineer. His imagination was fired by the French canal-building project, and he went to Panama to work on the canal. When de Lesseps' effort collapsed, Bunau-Varilla joined others in forming the New Panama Canal Company, which bought the equipment in the hopes of restarting the canal. He played an important role in getting the U.S. government to decide to build in Panama. After the project ended, Bunau-Varilla, then in his mid-fifties, fought for France during World War I. He lost a leg in one battle, but he survived and remained busy and energetic until his death.

13

Negotiating with Colombia

The United States still needed to lease the land for the canal from Colombia. The U.S. government offered to pay a sum of $10 million in advance and then another $250,000 each year, but the Senate of Colombia turned down the offer in 1903. U.S. president Theodore Roosevelt, who was determined to build the canal, was furious with the Colombians who had spoiled his plan.

Rebellion in Panama

Soon, however, another opportunity arose. The people of Panama had rebelled many times against Colombia's control of their land. They now saw a chance to break free of Colombia with American help. The Americans did not want to support a **revolution** openly, but they secretly showed the Panamanian rebels that they approved of the idea.

HELD UP THE WRONG MAN

The Colombians turned down the American offer because they thought it wasn't enough money. A 1903 cartoon shows President Roosevelt refusing to give in to Colombia's demands for more.

Man with a Plan
"A MAN A PLAN A CANAL, PANAMA."

*A famous **palindrome** about Theodore Roosevelt and the Panama Canal*

On November 3, 1903, Panamanian rebels declared their nation's independence. Colombian troops arrived to stop the rebellion, but the rebellion's supporters seized the Colombian officers and then paid the Colombian soldiers not to fight. U.S. warships were already waiting in the area. The next day, U.S. troops landed to make sure there was no fighting.

The Treaty with Panama

Within days, the United States recognized the government of Panama. Bunau-Varilla wrote a new treaty giving the United States the right—for $10 million—to build a canal in an area called the Canal Zone (see the map on page 27). The treaty also gave the United States **sovereignty** over the Canal Zone.

The Panamanians were angry with Bunau-Varilla for giving away sovereignty, but they accepted the treaty because they needed the $10 million offered by the United States. On November 18, 1903, Bunau-Varilla and U.S. Secretary of State John Hay signed the treaty.

Panama declared its independence from Colombia in 1903. This photograph shows Panamanians celebrating Independence Day in Panama City in 1911.

Chapter Three

Building the Canal

As workers (above) cleared land to build the canal, the debris was taken away by the railroad. In 1906, President Roosevelt (seen below standing inside a **steam shovel**) traveled to Panama to inspect progress on the canal. He told the engineers, "This is one of the great works of the world."

The Chiefs

In 1904, President Roosevelt appointed seven men to serve on the Isthmian Canal Commission (ICC). The ICC took control of the Canal Zone.

In 1905, engineer John Stevens became chief engineer of the Panama Canal project. He knew a good railroad system was important for moving millions of tons of dirt from the canal route. His first task, therefore, was to replace the old, small Panama Railroad with many more and stronger tracks. In the end, the rail system included 450 miles (724 km) of track.

In 1907, army engineer George Goethals replaced Stevens as the project's leader. He proved to be an able leader and was extremely careful with money. President Roosevelt, who took a personal interest in the project, gave Goethals complete control over the canal construction and over the seven-man ICC.

The Workers

About 75 percent of the workers were West Indians, most of them from Jamaica or Barbados. They did much of the heavy manual labor. The next largest group, the Americans, made up about 15 percent of the workers. The rest came from European countries—mostly Italy and Spain—or more than forty other nations, including India. At one point, the ICC had more than forty thousand workers.

Fighting Fever on the Panama Canal

A worker sprays a ditch to kill mosquitoes.

The United States sent an army doctor, William Gorgas, to try and solve the terrible problems of malaria and yellow fever. Gorgas set teams to work clearing the land on either side of the canal. They dug nearly 2,000 miles (3,200 km) of ditches so that swamps could be drained. Gorgas also ordered a coating of oil to be spread on areas of water to smother the mosquitoes that hatched from eggs laid on the water's surface. The teams also developed a spray that was used to kill newly hatched mosquitoes. In the cities, Gorgas's men paved streets to get rid of pools of water where female mosquitoes laid eggs. By December 1905, yellow fever was gone from Panama. Malaria rates dropped dramatically, from 205 cases in the period 1907–1908 to only 14 in the period 1913–1914.

These men were drilling holes to place dynamite for blasting through rock. Their task was one of many dangerous jobs that needed to be carried out on the canal.

The Dangers of Work

Far fewer workers died during the U.S. canal project than during the French effort, although the numbers were still high. About 5,600 people died while working on the U.S. project. A large number of workers died from pneumonia in 1907, but after that, construction accidents were the main threat to the lives of laborers.

Inequality in the Workforce

Workers were treated differently depending on where they came from. American workers were paid in U.S. gold dollars, while the rest were paid in silver dollars from Panama.

Having Fun

The ICC provided entertainment for higher-paid workers. The commission built clubhouses, dance halls, libraries, billiard rooms, and bowling alleys. The ICC also brought in movies and performers from the United States. In addition, it set aside land where workers could play baseball.

Americans filled the more advanced positions and had the highest wages, but European laborers still earned more than the West Indians did.

American workers had decent housing to live in and could eat in real dining halls. Europeans ate in food tents, and the West Indians were fed out of kitchen shacks. Unlike the whites, black workers had to provide their own housing, which was of poor quality because of the low wages they earned.

Different Jobs

Most workers labored on building the canal, but there were countless other jobs. Some built and maintained the houses and other buildings needed by the vast workforce. Others moved supplies in and around the Canal Zone. Some worked on the medical staff or did administrative work.

Cooks provided volumes of food for the canal workers, including six million loaves of bread in one year. Some cooking was done over campfires near where the men were working.

The Sounds of Hard Work
". . . the strident clink, clink of the drills eating their way into the rock; . . . the constant and uninterrupted rumble that told of the dirt trains ever plying over the crowded tracks; the heavy crash that accompanied the dumping of a six-ton boulder onto a flat car; the clanking of chains and the creaking of machinery as the arms of the steam shovels swung around looking for another load; the cries of men, and the booming of blasts."

Willis John Abbot, Panama and the Canal in Picture and Prose, *1913*

The Panama
Canal goes
right through
Gatún Lake
(above),
the largest
man-made
lake in the
world when
it was
formed. The
canal passes
the giant
Gatún Dam
(below right).
Both the dam
and the lake
were created
as part of the
canal-building
project.

Damming the River

The first construction task was to **dam** the wild Chagres River, near the Atlantic end of the canal. If this wasn't done, the area's heavy rains would turn the river into a raging force that would endanger ships using the canal. Gatún Dam was huge—1.5 miles (2.4 km) long, 0.5 miles (0.8 km) thick at the bottom, and tapering to 30 feet (9 meters) at the top.

The dam created a huge lake called Gatún Lake. The dam also provided power. A **hydroelectric** power plant built near the dam used the river to make electrical power. This energy would power the locks, the electric trains used to pull ships through the locks, and all the lights needed in the Canal Zone.

The Culebra Cut

Another big challenge was to carve a route for the canal through the Culebra highlands, situated toward the Pacific side of the isthmus. On this 9-mile (14-km) stretch of the canal, heavy rains often washed dirt from the highlands down onto the work area and threatened to doom the project.

The Americans had to make the Culebra **Cut** 1,800 feet (550 m) wide at the top, much wider than the width they actually needed for the canal. That way they could take away enough dirt to prevent mud slides into the canal.

Using Technology

To dig out all that dirt, the workers used high-powered steam shovels. When they hit solid rock, they used dynamite to blast it apart. Dirt and rock was carried away by the railroad. The material taken from the Culebra Cut was put to good use. Rock taken from Culebra was dumped into the oceans beyond the two canal entrances to help build **breakwaters**. Dirt from the cut was used to build the huge Gatún Dam.

A Great Spectacle

"He who did not see the Culebra Cut during the mighty work of excavation missed one of the great spectacles of all ages. . . . From its crest on a working day you looked down upon a mighty rift in the earth's crust, at the base of which pigmy engines and ant-like forms were rushing to and fro without seeming plan or reason."

Willis John Abbot, Panama and the Canal in Picture and Prose, *1913*

Building the Locks

Another crucial task was building the locks that
would allow ships to move between different
water levels. Each lock was huge—110 feet
(33.5 m) wide and 1,100 feet (335 m) long, or
the length of five city blocks. The locks' sides
soared to the height of a six-story building.

The bottom and sides of the locks were
made of concrete, poured on the site. Nothing
had ever been made of concrete on that scale
before, but the builders of the Panama Canal
made twelve of the huge structures. The steel
gates for the locks, weighing 400 tons (360
metric tons) or more, were made in the United
States and shipped to Panama to be installed.

The first
concrete
was poured
for the
Gatún Locks
in 1909.
Work on the
twelve locks
continued
until 1913.

Completing the Work

Workers finished the locks on the Pacific side first, followed by Gatún Locks on the Atlantic side. In June 1913, they completed the dam, and Gatún Lake was finally filled. In September of that year, the locks were tested and ready to go. The work on Culebra Cut was finished in December.

How the Locks Work

The Panama Canal has six pairs of locks in which water levels change so that ships can be raised or lowered between waterways of different heights. A ship that needs to be raised goes into the lock at the lower level, and the gates are closed. Then the lock is filled with enough water to raise the water level—and the ship—to the higher level. The gates open, and the ship continues along the canal at the higher level. A ship coming the other way goes into the lock and waits while some of the water is drained out. The ship descends as the water drains, until it is level with the lower canal and can continue on its way.

Small electric engines, called "mules," run alongside each lock and pull ships through the lock system with towing cables.

Chapter Four

Using the Canal

On opening day, August 15, 1914, the *Ancon* entered the Pedro Miguel Locks on its way to the Pacific Ocean.

A Quiet Journey

"So quietly did [the *Ancon*] pursue her way that . . . a strange observer coming suddenly upon the scene would have thought that the canal had always been in operation, and that the *Ancon* was only doing what thousands of other vessels must have done before her."

John Barrett, "The Opening of the Panama Canal," 1914

Opening Ceremonies

On August 15, 1914, the Panama Canal officially opened when the *Ancon*, a cargo ship, made the journey along it. The ship carried various officials, including Panama's president and the U.S. ambassador. Chief engineer George Goethals was not on board. He rode on the train line alongside the canal, stopping at each lock to make sure everything was in order before the ship arrived. The ship made the trip in less than ten hours.

Path between the Seas

Ten years or so after it opened, the Panama Canal was handling five thousand ships a year.

Pilots take over vessels while they are still in the deep waters at either end of the canal. Pilots have complete control throughout the journey.

By the 1970s, about fifteen thousand ships were traveling the canal each year, as lights were installed and ships were allowed to make the journey at night. That number works out to be a rate of nearly two ships per hour every day of the year.

Traveling the Canal

When ships prepare to enter the canal, their captains must hand over the steering to pilots. These experienced workers are very important on the canal. They guide the ships along the channel from one end of the canal to the other and in and out of the locks.

Twists and Turns

"The canal is so short, with great variables in tides on the Pacific side and with so many narrow twists and turns, such sudden changes in weather and wind, that if I look away for even three seconds, we could be out of the channel and on a sandbar."

Pilot Edgar Tejada, on steering ships through the canal, 1999

Conclusion

Change of Ownership

When the United States began building the canal, it was just beginning to play a powerful role in the world. Completing this work helped give Americans new confidence in their abilities and power.

Many Panamanians, however, remained angry over the terms of the 1903 treaty. In 1977, Panama and the United States finally agreed that the United States would continue operating the canal only until the end of 1999. Then Panama would take control of the canal, and all U.S. military forces would leave the Canal Zone. The handover took place on December 31, 1999.

The transfer of the Panama Canal from U.S. to Panamanian control took place in 1999. This photograph shows the ceremonial handover.

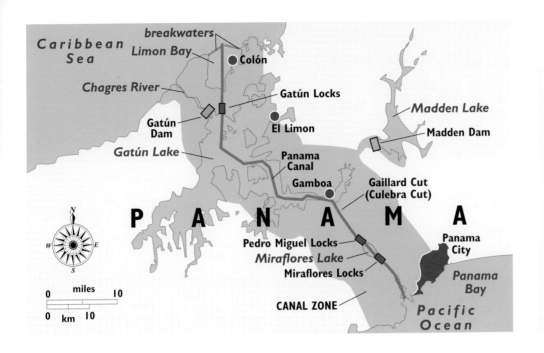

This map shows the area of the Canal Zone as well as various sites along the Panama Canal.

Improvements

The canal today is different than when it was completed in 1914. In the 1930s, another dam—the Madden Dam—was built, east of the canal. This dam helps control the flow of water into Gatún Lake and generates extra electricity. In the 1970s and again in the 1990s, the Culebra Cut—now named the Gaillard Cut—was made broader and deeper. As a result, the largest ships that go through the canal can now pass each other in the cut.

Fewer Ships

The Panama Canal increased trade and wealth for many countries by making the transportation of goods so much cheaper than before. In saving thousands of miles of travel, shippers can save thousands of dollars.

Since the 1970s, when traffic on the Panama Canal reached its busiest point, use of the canal has fallen. More and more ships have been built that are too large to fit in the locks. Still, about twelve thousand ships a year travel along the Panama Canal, and it remains one of the world's vital waterways.

Taking Control
"I feel very, very happy that my country's finally becoming whole again, that we're going to be a sovereign, a free nation, that we're not going to have any more foreign troops in Panama, and I think that the future is a challenge, but the Panamanian people are . . . up to it."

Juan Carlos Navarro, mayor of Panama City, 1999

Time Line

1846	U.S. treaty with Colombia gives the United States the right to move people and goods across the isthmus of Panama.
1855	Panama Railroad is completed.
1879	Ferdinand de Lesseps holds a conference to discuss Central American canal.
1880	French effort to dig the canal begins.
1889	French canal company declares bankruptcy.
1902	U.S. Senate approves canal route in Panama.
1903	August 2: Colombia rejects treaty for Panama Canal.
	November 3: Panama declares independence.
	November 6: United States recognizes Panama's independence.
	November 18: Hay-Bunau-Varilla treaty gives United States the right to build Panama Canal.
1904	May 2: United States buys holdings of New Panama Canal Company of France.
	May 5: Panama hands Canal Zone over to United States.
1905	John Stevens is appointed chief engineer of Panama Canal project.
1907	George Goethals replaces Stevens as head of the project.
1909	First concrete floor is laid for Gatún Locks.
1913	Work is completed on locks, Gatún Dam, and Culebra Cut.
1914	August 15: Panama Canal officially opens.
1977	United States agrees to return the Panama Canal to Panama in 1999.
1999	Panama takes control of the Panama Canal.

Things to Think About and Do

Building the Canal

Imagine you have gone to Panama to work on the construction of the canal in the early 1900s. Write about your experiences there—your work, how you lived, the people you met, and the challenges of the different land and climate.

The Impact of the Canal

Before the days of trains, trucks, and airplanes, people depended much more on the world's waterways for moving goods from one place to another. Although we have other means of transportation today, ships are still used for carrying large, heavy cargoes over long distances. Take a look at a map of the world, and think about the routes ships would have taken before the Panama Canal was built. What countries have been helped most by the canal's existence? Then find the Suez Canal in Egypt, and think about how that canal must have affected shipping routes in other parts of the world.

Glossary

bankruptcy: state in which a company loses control of its finances and property because it has so many debts.

breakwater: barrier built in the sea near a harbor to block high waves from entering the harbor.

canal: man-made waterway.

cut: man-made or natural channel carved through land.

dam: stop or control the flow of water; and the structure that stops and controls a river's flow, often creating a man-made lake.

debris: trash, remains, or leftover pieces; often used to mean broken pieces of rock.

hydroelectric: electrical energy generated by using the force of flowing water.

lock: mechanism in a canal that allows boats to be raised or lowered from a body of water at one level to another body of water at a higher or lower level.

palindrome: word or phrase that is spelled the same both forward and backward.

revolution: overthrowing of a government and setting up of a new system of government.

sovereignty: right to rule over an area of land.

steam shovel: machine that uses steam power to dig soil and rock out of the ground.

technology: knowledge and ability that improves ways of doing practical things.

treaty: agreement made between two or more people or groups, usually after negotiation.

Further Information

Books

English, Peter (ed.). *Panama in Pictures* (Visual Geography Series). Lerner, 1996.

Harness, Cheryl. *Young Teddy Roosevelt*. National Geographic, 1998.

Mann, Elizabeth. *The Panama Canal* (Wonders of the World). Mikaya, 1998.

Nobleman, Marc Tyler. *Panama* (Countries of the World). Bridgestone, 2002.

Parker, Nancy Winslow. *Locks, Crocs, and Skeeters: The Story of the Panama Canal*. Morrow, William and Co., 1996.

Winkelman, Barbara Gaines. *The Panama Canal* (Cornerstones of Freedom). Children's Press, 1999.

Web Sites

www.pancanal.com Official Web site of the organization that runs the canal has information on its current operations.

www.sil.si.edu/Exhibitions/Make-the-Dirt-Fly/ Smithsonian Institution Web site has great information and images explaining the building of the canal.

www.theodoreroosevelt.org Web site devoted to the life and achievements of President Theodore Roosevelt.

Useful Addresses

The Panama Canal Museum
7985 113th Street
Suite 100
Seminole, FL 33772-4785
Telephone: (727) 394-9338

Index